T0209380

Sacred Inner Trails

Meditative Journeys from Heartbreak to
Wholeness with Workbook for Self or Group Study

CHRISTINE CHIECHI

BALBOA.PRESS
A DIVISION OF HAY HOUSE

Balboa Press books may be ordered through booksellers or by contacting:

Balboa Press
A Division of Hay House
1663 Liberty Drive
Bloomington, IN 47403
www.balboapress.com
1 (877) 407-4847

Because of the dynamic nature of the Internet, any web addresses or links contained in this book may have changed since publication and may no longer be valid. The views expressed in this work are solely those of the author and do not necessarily reflect the views of the publisher, and the publisher hereby disclaims any responsibility for them.

The author of this book does not dispense medical advice or prescribe the use of any technique as a form of treatment for physical, emotional, or medical problems without the advice of a physician, either directly or indirectly. The intent of the author is only to offer information of a general nature to help you in your quest for emotional and spiritual well-being. In the event you use any of the information in this book for yourself, which is your constitutional right, the author and the publisher assume no responsibility for your actions.

Any people depicted in stock imagery provided by Getty Images are models, and such images are being used for illustrative purposes only. Certain stock imagery © Getty Images.

Print information available on the last page.

ISBN: 978-1-9822-4735-5 (sc)
ISBN: 978-1-9822-4737-9 (hc)
ISBN: 978-1-9822-4736-2 (e)

Library of Congress Control Number: 2020908468

Balboa Press rev. date: 05/07/2020

Contents

Introduction vii

Going Gently into This New Year 1
    Embracing the New, Releasing the Old, Setting a New Rhythm

Rebuilding from the Ruins 13
    Restoration, Wholeness, and Rising from the Rubble

Starlight Canvas 21
    Painting a Bright New Future

Spring Awakening 29
    Hope, Promise, Renewal

Hot Air Balloon 37
    Freeing Ourselves, Cutting the Cords That Bind Us

Lotus Flower 45
    From Suffering Comes Beauty

Rolling Waves 53
    Trust, Surrender, Courage

Lighthouse 61
    You Are a Beacon of Light and Hope

Sanctuary of Stillness 69
    Stillness, Wisdom, Connecting with Source

Loosening the Blanket of Security 79
    Trusting Self, Letting Go

Along a Pebbly Beach 89
    Going with the Flow, Everything is Temporary, Acceptance

Into Fullness...97
    Wholeness, Fulfillment

Autumn Grace...105
    Letting Go, Courage

Winter's Growing Light.......................................111
    Year's End, Staying in the Growing Light

About the Author...121

Introduction

As I battled to survive the most important and heartbreaking challenge of my life, I sought out healing and strength through the meditations I wrote and the outdoor trails I hiked. This book was birthed from the union of these, and it was how I took my personal adventure from heartbreak and despair into a new sense of wholeness.

When I first set out to heal myself, I was smack dab in the middle of the biggest and heart-wrenching challenge of my life. Each day, in order to keep myself strong and centered, I took long hikes with my dog, Kahlua, in desperate search of healing. I went to the beach, the woods, the farms, somewhere, anywhere quiet in nature where I could be among something greater than myself, clear my mind, focus on what I needed to heal, and make a plan to move forward.

One day, while writing a meditation for a class, I realized each meditation I was writing was a hike I had taken, and each hike in turn was a meditation waiting to be written. Through this realization, the two came together, and thus this book.

I was able to bring healing not only to myself but also to so many others who attended my weekly mediation and Reiki classes. Every week for two years, I held Reiki circles and led mediation groups with people like myself down the sacred inner trails into wholeness. I was delighted to see the very positive response to my meditations and how the seeds for healing in others were being watered week after week.

How to Use This Book

This book is like a map leading to one destination, a sense of renewed purpose and well-being. In life, there are many different paths one can take that lead to the same destination. With that in mind, there is no one right place to begin. The book starts at New Year's Day and ends at winter solstice, so you can pick up the book any time of the year.

Whether using it for self-study or for a group class, thumb through the table of contents and choose a journey that resonates with you for that day or that time of year. Choose what feels right at the time.

Each journey in this book puts you along the trail to healing in four parts.

Packing Your Spiritual Backpack
Setting Out/Relaxation Techniques
The Journey
Journey's End Reward

Packing Your Spiritual Backpack

Like with many hikes, each meditative journey or trail in this book begins with packing a backpack. The participant will pack the spiritual backpack with things to contemplate before setting out along the trail.

These include questions like:
"What aspect of healing will I explore today? Of forgiveness? Of letting go? Of replenishment?"

"What challenges am I currently experiencing, and how are the affecting me?"

Relaxation Techniques and Setting Out

This section of the experience relaxes and soothes participants by helping them prepare mentally, physically, and spiritually for whatever may pop up emotionally along the trail. The relaxation through breathing, visualization, and positive words aids in letting go and building inner strength and courage to take the journey into healing.

The Journey

Each meditation leads you down a trail into self-realization. The journeys or trails lead to letting go, accepting, trusting, having faith, and recovery and renewal. Each takes participants to a place where they can rest, regroup, and make a plan on how to move forward.

Journey's End Reward

Every journey, no matter how difficult, has its rewards.

At the conclusion of every trail taken, the participants will be softly taken back from their inner world into the present moment. They are asked to write their responses to questions such as:

"What benefits did I receive in taking this journey?"

"What revelations have I discovered about myself? My situation? Others?"

And very important, "What steps can I take next to help me heal into wholeness?"

Author's Hope

Every meditation is a version of an actual experience I have had along the journey back to myself. Each was written to illustrate what I saw, felt, and explored in attempting to heal for that day. These journeys have been very well received by hundreds of people, and it is my hope they will set as many people as possible on a positive trail to healing.

Blessings to you. Enjoy the journey back to wholeness!

For my daughter, Danielle.
My heart, my meaning in life.

Going Gently into This New Year

Embracing the New, Releasing the Old, Setting a New Rhythm

With every new year, we are given the blessing of starting again. We have the opportunity to plot a new course and set a new rhythm for ourselves going forward. Confidently and without hesitation, we can gently journey into the unknown wonders of the new year.

The new year invites us to release the old, let it go, and make room for new blessings to come in great abundance not only for ourselves but for all others.

Packing Your Spiritual Backpack

What do I wish to release from this past year?
What experiences?
What pain?
What misfortune?

_____

_____

_____

_____

What would it feel like to set a completely new and different rhythm for this year?

_____

_____

_____

_____

What new things would I like to make room for in the coming year?

_____

_____

_____

_____

Setting Out
Relaxation

Open your hands on your lap;
Let your shoulders go loose and limp.
Release any strain from your neck, back, and jaw, and just be.

Become mindful of your breath,
That easy flow of in and out.
Let it soothe you into comfort as your body lets go.
Let it lull you inward as your mind clears and quiets.

Breathe away all the old.
Gather it up with your breath and release with one forceful exhale.
Feel it bit by bit, letting go of you as you let go of it,
Freeing yourself from the past by
Breathing it away in a willingly release.
Surrender it all and
Watch it float far, far away.

Be still.
Breathe in the new …
A new energy that is being birthed in this very moment.
Being birthed from letting go and making room.
Embrace this new energy as you inhale.
Draw it in and feel it,
Clean and clear.
New energy is now circulating through you.
This is an energy of possibility and of hope.

Relax and settle deep into this newness.
Become quiet and calm.
Receive and just be.
Finding now a beautiful new rhythm growing within.

A new rhythm in your breath …
One that belongs solely to you.
Follow that sensation of newness.

A new and natural ebb and flow …
Let your new breath now set the course for this new year …

Relax deeply into this new rhythm.
Let its softness calm you
And take you further inward …

Journey

Allow a serene and peaceful woodland setting to unfold in your mind, one where tall pine trees that touch the sky line your path and fill the air with a scent that lifts your soul. As your guide for a long time, this path has brought you to experience great beauty and has led you to incredible places.

The landscape around you is breathtaking, yet your mind and body are tired from a journey long traveled. You are taking your very last steps along this path as it finally comes to an end on the banks of a gently flowing river.

Here, you rest your feet, taking time now to relax and recenter.

You sit at the path's end, watching the gentle water of the river flow at your feet. Upstream, a majestic mountain stands tall and strong under a bright blue sky. As the snow melts from the mountaintop, it cascades down into the river, carrying with it the energies of the past year and the trail you traveled to be here.

You have experienced so much this past year. There have been joyous moments and memorable times. Yet along with the good, there have also been challenges. These challenges have taken their toll on you and left their mark in the form of energy you wish to wash yourself clean of before the new year.

Looking to the mountain, you imagine the melting snow carrying the energies of those challenges, hardships, and pain. They run down the mountainside and empty into the river below. The water becomes dark and muddy as they roll into the river, and you simply watch with no attachment as the murky water flows by you.

This river is a symbol of all that is old and no longer serving. You think of all those things you wish to release from the past year and watch them float by your feet. Within the murky water lies the images and residue of all you are releasing. They flow by, making their way downstream and out of sight. You watch as the river picks up its pace and runs more quickly by you.

Taking a deep breath in, you pull up any last bit of muddy residue left over in your body from the past year and blow it out into the river, letting it all go. All the pain, disappointment, and sorrow are being released through your breath and are being taken downstream and out of sight.

Watch until it all completely flows out of sight,

until the river flows crystal clear,
until the river flows fresh and clean.

The river's current soon changes.
It flows at a more gentle and easy pace.

You breathe in the pine-scented air and feel renewed. You, like the flow of the water, sit light and gentle in your energy. You can breathe softer now. The energy of the past is gone and out of sight. Your breath now flows crystal clear just like this mountain river, and you can delight in beginning anew.

With a clear mind and heart, you concentrate now on the rhythm and flow of your breath. Breathing in and out, soft and gentle, relaxed and rhythmic, feeling the peace and flow. Roll with your breath. With every rise of your breath, there is a fall, with every ebb a flow. Feel yourself easily moving within that flow of rise and fall. Ride with the ups and downs of your own breath, the ins and outs. Sit soft and tranquil, breathing now with no effort at all.

Through your breath, you become connected with a unique new rhythm of this new year. Let your mind be a clean and clear space in which to dwell. Feel your surroundings become more peaceful and comforting, allowing you to settle deeper into this peace. And let your entire being be at ease. With your breath, you are setting the pace and rhythm of the year to come. Through your mindfulness of breath and heart, you are going gently into this new year.

Sitting beside the river, you look upstream to the majestic mountain. This mountain is a symbol of the grandeur of your potential in the new year. All that has yet to be accomplished, experienced, and felt exists in the symbol of this mountain.

It represents the blessings and the gifts and all that is possible. You look again to the river as it flows crystal clear. This is your river, your flow of life in the coming year, your very life force within.

Follow with your eyes the gentle flow of water as it makes its way downstream. When you feel comfortable, get up and slowly step into it water. Ease your feet in and notice how the water flows gently and clear around your ankles and legs. Take notice of the current moving slowly, softly, naturally, and without effort.

And now begin to journey downstream, walking easily through the sand and tiny stones beneath your feet. Know that these are your first steps of this new year.

Notice how effortlessly you walk through the water.
Notice the nature all around you in peace and harmony.
As you journey downstream, along the shore you can see images of the possibilities to come in the new year.

All that you desire and all that is to come is being revealed to you on the banks of the river.

What is it that you see coming for you in the new year?

What situations of personal success? What accomplishments?

See the new gifts, new blessings, new people and places that are coming your way in the new year.
Take it all in.

With each step downstream, feel yourself moving at ease with the flow of river.

Gently, you are walking your first steps into these new year's blessings.

Soon the current of the river becomes a little faster, but still slow enough to walk through safely. No matter how fast the current flows, you continue to walk within it safely, with strength and with ease.

There are rocks and stones of all sizes in the river. You notice how the water flows, never allowing the rocks to deter it. And like the water, you too do not let them deter you. You simply make your way over them and around them. No matter how large the stones, you make your way over them easily, with strength and grace, remembering as you walk that the water is the flow of life and you will walk this coming new year confidently as it flows, fast or slow.

The stones and rocks are the challenges you will face. But with grace and ease, you walk through each challenge, no matter how big.

Soon the current slows to a softer pace, and you feel more confident than ever.

You come to where the water has stilled and has emptied into a shimmering lake. Tall trees and nature surround the lake in all their beauty.

There is a serene stillness in this moment that eases your soul. The sunlight shines strong and bright, like your confidence. And there is quiet knowing that all is well.

Looking back upstream, you can see the great mountain in the distance. In its majesty, you can feel the pure possibility of what lies ahead for you this year. You have the strength of the mountain to endure and succeed this year. You have the will of the water to flow gently and with grace through all of the new year.

You watch the water as it flows into the lake from upstream. As it flows, the water brings with it gift upon gift, presents in pretty bows flowing toward you in abundance. An unlimited supply of unopened presents from the universe, there to symbolize that there is no limit to the blessings that will come.

So receive and let these blessings in pretty packages flow to you and surround you. Rejoice with a grateful heart as you reach out your arms and give thanks in advance to the universe for what is on its way.

Today, the first day of new and great possibilities, you choose one gift to open. This gift will set the tone for the year to come. You excitedly open it, you understand it, and you cherish it. Receive this blessing and give thanks.

In gratitude for the many blessing to come, you begin to think,
What will be the gifts that I give to others this coming year?
Where will I give love?
Where will I be helpful and charitable?
How will I help others to feel deserving and worthy?
How will I gift joy?

Think now of the unique gifts you will give to others. You now gather a few unopened packages and carry them with you as you step out of the lake. These are gifts you will decide to give away, gifts you will share gifts you will give to others so they too can experience love, joy, happiness, and success.

Take these gifts with you and make them very tiny … Place them in your pocket by your heart and know they are always there for you to share …

Journey's End Reward

Stepping out of the lake, you can see a path of glistening light emerging from the surrounding forest. This is your path forward into the new year. When you are ready, say goodbye this beautiful place and give thanks. Take your first steps on that path of light with optimism and confidence. Step gently yet boldly and with purpose onto this path of the new year. Set your pace as you follow the path of light each and every day to come.

Feel the light energy from the path soak into your feet. Your path forward will be by this light. Feel it run up your legs to give you strength. Feel it run into your heart, making every step forward a step directed by love. Breathe and bring the light back as you move softly back to the present. Come gently back into the room ready now to experience all the grandeur of this new year with gratitude and a gentle spirit.

How did it feel to confidently and safely walk through the large rocks in the river?

_____

_____

_____

_____

How does your new rhythm for this year feel differently?

_____

_____

_____

_____

What gift was your first gift that set the tone for this year and what does it mean to you?

_____

_____

_____

_____

What are the new possibilities you saw for the coming new year?

_____

_____

_____

_____

What gift will you be giving to others this year and what does it symbolize?

_____

_____

_____

_____

Rebuilding from the Ruins

Restoration, Wholeness, and
Rising from the Rubble

Time and situations can take their toll emotionally and physically, leaving us in pieces like rubble. With self-forgiveness, commitment, and a belief in ourselves, we can learn it is never too late to rise from the rubble and rebuild.

Packing Your Spiritual Backpack

What situation do you feel has left you in pieces?

_____

_____

_____

_____

What pieces of yourself are in need of restoration and rebuilding?

_____

_____

_____

_____

What would it take to feel whole again?

_____

_____

_____

_____

Setting Out
Relaxation

Close your eyes and breathe deeply.
Exhale fully and let go.
Invite yourself to pause, to be still.
Breathe, and just be …

Feel your breath run through you like warm white light.
Let the light enter your body, bringing you to peace and
Giving you permission to just let go …

Your physical body relaxes.
Any aches, any pains gently release themselves.
Your emotional body becomes calm
As your mind settles down and welcomes in the quiet.

Drift now into a serene and blissful calm.
Drift now into rest.
Slip away further within as the white light washes over your entire
being
And your body gives into the peace.

The outside world gently disappears
As you dwell in the presence of pure white light.

Tiny sparkles of light flow towards you from above, floating down
like warm snow.
They softly touch your face, your cheeks and head.
Their warmth opens you to you sink deeper and trust.

These sparkles of light float down past you
And pile up on the ground at your feet
Illuminating the ground all around you.
The earth is blanketed in this soft white light;
Like snow, it stretches out over a beautiful countryside setting.
Here it is quiet. Here there is peace.

Journey

Green hills of grass roll out like waves at your feet. The earth beneath you is firm and supportive, grounding you on your journey through a picturesque countryside. A calming blue sky brings you a sense of peace, and the fresh feeling in the air stirs your spirit.

You follow a trail along the landscape up and over the many small hills, enjoying your walk. At the base of one hill, you notice pieces of stone curiously scattered all over the ground. Carefully and respectfully, you walk around the stones, noticing details and images curiously carved into their surfaces. They appear to be part of what was once a beautiful and meaningful place but now lay crumbling on the ground at your feet.

You follow the stones upward to the top of the hill. Here, you come to the sight of a magnificent, ancient ruin. You are awestruck by its presence and intrigued by its energy. These ruins exude a magical and mysterious spirit, very much alive, that draws you closer.

Walking forward, you come to crumbling stairs that lead you to worn stone pillars. They stand tall and tower over you, and their presence suggests this is a place of great importance. You enter the structure and feel a profound wisdom that emanates from its once stable walls.

As you walk around, you cannot help but imagine what this place must have been like when first built. So full of mystery and yet sadness.

A cry for deep healing seems to calls out amid all this broken beauty. Time and situations have taken a toll on this once strong and beautiful structure and scattered it in pieces on the ground where you stand. There is an unmistakable yearning in the air, one that cries out to be whole again.

On some level, you can relate to this structure and empathize as it stands in pieces.

You too have been affected by time and situations. You can recall where in your life the pieces of yourself have been scattered and worn down. and you too yearn to be whole again.

You look to the ruins spread out along broken floor inside; some will be easy to put together, and some will be difficult. But with empathy and determination, you respectfully answer the call to rebuild.

Gathering the pieces one by one, you begin to slowly rebuild. As you restore the structure, you are restoring and rebuilding yourself. Putting the pieces back together, recalling what they are for you.

As you pick each piece and put them back into place, you reflect on how you are mending pieces of yourself. Each piece is something you are reclaiming as your own, putting it all back in its rightful place, you are healing and making yourself whole again.

Some pieces are heavier than others and at times difficult to mend, but you persevere, laying even the tiniest pieces back in place, so carefully and with so much love.

You reflect on what needs restoration and rebuilding in your own life. And what you can do to bring a sense of wholeness to your life. When the last little piece is put back in place, you stand back behold the structure in its grandness, its beauty, and smile.

You walk amid the restoration and feel your own grandeur. Your own sense of wholeness, your love of self. You lay your hands on the wall of the structure and feel its gratitude. You exchange energy of strength and a newfound confidence to stand tall. You thank the structure for what it has taught you today and make your way down the now mended stone stairs. In rebuilding this structure, you have begun restoring yourself into wholeness.

You step back from the structure and make your way down the mended stairs. Walking down the hill, you follow the grass as the sky opens up and light sparkles begin to fall. They touch your face and fill the ground all around you, and once again you stand in a white light landscape.

Journey's End Reward

The light softly brings you back to this moment in time,
Back to this sacred space,
Back to the here and now,
Feeling refreshed and renewed

And with a greater sense of well-being and wholeness.
Go in peace.

In what way did you relate to the structure when you first saw it in pieces?

_____

_____

_____

_____

What can you do for yourself right now that will help restore a sense of wholeness in yourself?

_____

_____

_____

_____

Starlight Canvas

Painting a Bright New Future

We tend to physically and mentally carry with us the energies of heartbreak and disappointment for long after the situation is done. We believe they keep us safe, but in reality they are heavy and wear us down. The weight of carrying these energies around holds us back and keeps us in the past, preventing any healing from actually occurring. At the moment we decide to put down that weight, we can begin to heal, move forward, and create a picture of a bright new future.

Packing Your Spiritual Backpack

What weight from personal challenges are you still carrying?

_____

_____

_____

_____

What do you believe are the benefits from continuing to carry this weight?

_____

_____

_____

_____

How is carrying this weight preventing you physically and emotionally from stepping onto a new path?

_____

_____

_____

_____

Setting Out
Relaxation

Breathe,
and feel the weight of the world slowly drop away
Breathe,
and feel the day, the week, the month gently fade …

There is nothing for you to do,
there is no place for you to be … here and now is all there is.

So relax, put your attention on your breath, and let go.
Become very still
and gently ease yourself into a peaceful state of relaxation.
Notice how good it feels to just let your body go …
As you breathe, your mind clears and becomes very quiet.
You feel lighter and lighter
and more at ease.
Allowing yourself now to just be.

Journey

Imagine it is dusk, and you are walking along the shore of a sparkling blue ocean. You watch as the sun sets slowly over the water and brings a shimmer to its surface.

It is a very blissful evening. All is quiet and peaceful along this shore. As you walk, you look over your shoulder and watch the waves gently wash away the footprints left behind in the sand.

It has been a long, long journey. One where you have traveled a great distance.

The soft sand soothes your sore feet, and you yearn to put down the heavy backpack weighing you down. You find a pretty spot on the beach to rest and watch as Mother Nature takes her paintbrush to the sky and unveils a brilliant sunset. The vibrant hues of red, yellow, and orange comfort you as she paints. You breathe in the grounding energies of red, the nurturing hues of orange, and the empowering glow of the yellow.

Here on the beach, there is finally time to rest and gather some relief after your long journey.

The sky is getting darker as the sun dips down under the horizon. You gather up any kindling you can find on the beach and set out to build a fire. When you are finished, you light the fire and rest in its warming glow.

The sky becomes very dark, but you feel safe and relaxed by the crackling fire.

On your feet are tattered shoes, worn by the steps of a long and sometimes difficult journey. Along the way, they have been like a comfortable and reliable companion, a true support. Examining them, you reflect on all you have walked through and experienced together. These shoes have protected your every step and moved you safely along life's unpredictable trails. They have experienced all the good and forged you forward though many struggles of the past.

Slipping them off, you think about what they symbolize for you and give thanks for their supportive role on your journey

You place your shoes beside you on the sand. The backpack on your shoulders is heavy. You have gathered and held on to so much throughout your journey and think about how it may be time to finally drop the weight of it all.

Carefully you slip off your heavy backpack, take a deep cleansing breathe, and feel the instant and welcoming relief. It feels so good to finally put down that weight. You unzip the backpack and begin sifting through all the stuff you have been carrying. One by one, you pull out objects that have weighed you down and reflect on each one's role along your journey.

Examining the objects, you think about what they represent and what energies they hold. Are they energies that feel light and joyful, or are they energies of disappointment? Sadness? Control? Whatever they represent, you can decide it is time to let them go and now declare you are ready to move on to something new.

You move the objects onto the sand, placing them next to your tattered shoes.

The fire continues to burn brightly in front of you. It is warm and gives you comfort in the dark night. You look back at the objects you took out of the backpack, knowing they no longer serve you. They have no place on your journey forward.

One by one, you pick them up and throw them into the fire. As you watch flames engulf them, you thank each one for what it was there to teach. A beautiful relief comes over you, and you feel free.

The sky has becomes very dark. You can feel safe and relaxed by the light of crackling fire. Feeling light and at ease, you take a nice, deep breath and feel the cooling evening air circulate throughout your body.

A vast and empty night sky hangs above you like a fresh new canvas. It is a night of the new moon. The perfect time to bring something new into your life.

You look to your tattered shoes and know you are ready to walk a brand-new path. You thank your shoes for all they have walked you through and with gratitude throw them into the fire, releasing them with love. Releasing all of the old and any old beliefs and feelings. Releasing all the fear, control, and disappointment.

While you watch them burn, you thank them for what they had come to teach and affirm you are ready for something new.

You reach into your backpack and pull out a brand-new pair of shoes. These new shoes will be your guide, your protection, your companion on your journey forward. With every new step you take, they will give you confidence as you blaze a new trail forward.

Slipping on the shoes, you notice how completely different they feel, and you are suddenly filled with optimism.

You gaze up into the empty, comforting sky. What new possibilities does the universe hold for you now? A clean fresh canvas hangs before you waiting for you to create any future you desire.

By letting go the weight of the old energy, you have given yourself the room to start anew and create a fresh beginning. You think about all you want the future to be, what trails you want to forge, and what opportunities you want to create.

For each thing you desire, a single star appears and lights up the evening sky, and this is exciting.

You think big, very big, bringing new and brighter stars to shimmer and light up the dark sky

The starlight now becomes your paintbrush, creating images and constellations in the sky that paint the picture of your future. You are free to create anything, so why not create big! You gaze upon the beautiful bright future you have painted with the stars. Optimism and excitement fills about your future fill you to the core.

After some time, the night begins to give way to a new morning. In your new shoes and with a lighter backpack, you set out along the shore, walking toward the rising sun. A brand-new day filled with hope is dawning.

Journey's End Reward

Walking into the rising sun, you begin to travel slowly back now to this space in time. Feeling lighter than when you started.

Bringing with you a new hope and sense of excitement for your future.

Gently returning.
Opening your eyes.
Begin to feel your body where you are,
breathe and
welcome back.

Describe what your tattered shoes symbolized about your journey.

_____

_____

_____

_____

What were the benefits from letting go of that weight?

_____

_____

_____

_____

How did your new shoes look and feel differently?

_____

_____

_____

_____

Draw or describe what you painted with the starlight. What new things are you creating?

_____

_____

_____

_____

Spring Awakening

Hope, Promise, Renewal

With spring, the time of promise, renewal and rebirth has arrived. As we shed the dark and challenging winter and all it symbolized, we transition into the new hopeful future of spring.

Packing Your Spiritual Backpack

What will you shed from this past winter? What challenges? What pain? What disappointments?

_____

_____

_____

_____

What are you hopeful for this spring?

_____

_____

_____

_____

Setting Out
Relaxation

Breathe in light.
Breathe out all that feels heavy.
Breathe in freedom.
Breathe out all the confines you.

Feel your belly rise and fall as you breathe.
Let your breath be comfortable and soothing.
Follow the soft sound of the in and out as it brings you ever inward.
And gently now drift into a soft state of relaxation.

Let your breath by your guide as it softly blows over mind like a gentle breeze … clearing your mind, taking away your worldly thoughts.
It blows over your body and loosens your body of any weight you carry from any stress or strain.

Now drift. Softly and smoothly away and inward.
Feel yourself shed the heaviness of this world
and become lighter and lighter.
Float and flutter in the tranquil light.
Feeling peaceful, weightless and at easy …

Journey

Deep within a forest, in a mystical and enchanted woods, you find yourself awakening in tiny little house much like that of a hobbit or gnome. Here, you have spent the winter, in quiet and in stillness and safe through harsh weather, darkness and the many challenges winter presents.

It has been a time of reflecting, on letting the darkness pass and waiting eagerly as the light outward and within was growing.

You are dressed in very warm and comforting clothing.

Each piece of clothing sheltered you through cold and darker times.

Each piece a reminder of the challenges you carried throughout winter.

With great anticipation, you have awaited arrival of spring. You look to your heavy clothing, no longer comfortable. Each article of clothing has served its purpose, and excitedly you begin to shed the clothing as if to be finally shedding the winter itself.

As you disrobe, you think of what you are shedding from the long winter. What disappointment, what challenges what dark and lonely times … You shed all that the winter was for you and immediately feel lighter. Dressed now more comfortably for the transition into spring.

Feeling lighter in your new clothing, you move through the tiny house to find the front door and peek outside. To your delight, you witness the long-awaited end of winter and give thanks.

The last small patches of snow are now melting on the mossy forest floor. The sunlight, as promised, stretches out its rays warmer and wider. Soft rays of light gleam through the trees and reach out to warm the forest floor below. You step out the doorway and give thanks to the tiny home for its shelter you take the first new breath of spring. As you breathe in your first breath of spring, you feel a noticeable and welcome shift in the energy.

In front of you, green moss emerges under the patches of melting snow, creating a path for you to follow. As you walk, the light from the sun shines to warm you, and all the forest is gleaming with its promise of hope, renewal, and regeneration.

In this mystical place, the trees grow very wide and very tall. Their roots spread out strong and thick over mossy ground, and all about them, woodland creatures scurry with joy. An excited rustle of magic fills the air in this enchanted land.

Taking the green moss path, you hike along through tall trees and mystical woodland sights. You follow the path as it winds through this enchanted land and the first signs of spring unfold. Any last bit of snow has now melted, and the promise of rebirth is apparent everywhere you look. Your heart fills with hope and optimistic anticipation as you journey forward.

The mossy green path leads to a clearing of grass surrounded by newly budded flowers and trees. In this clearing, you find a large stump of a once old, wise tree; here, you sit and take it all in. The tree stump is supportive beneath you, and the warmth of the sun shining through the trees upon your face stirs an awakening within you to all that is new.

You take off your shoes and feel the cool moss under your feet. You can feel the stirring of the energy of new life beneath. A loving green energy playfully greets you as it rises up through the earth and tickles your toes.

You sink your feet into the ground and acknowledge the rising energy of rebirth and renewal.

As you sit you reflect on what spring means for you and the promises that are present in its arrival, what do you desire most to be renewed and reawakened?

What hope do you hold for yourself and others?

What is the light that you have been waiting for as winter's darkness dwindles?

Through the soles of your feet, you can feel your desires leaving your body. You send them deep into the earth as if you are planting personal seeds of renewal and rebirth with your words. You send them deep into the soil below. You take note of what you are planting for yourself, for others, all of what you wish to be reborn ...

Feeling the earth now, receiving them and stirring the seeds of your desires with the energy of the promise of spring.

A fresh, new feeling begins to rise beneath you. Suddenly, up out of the earth, hundreds of tiny little fairies wake from beneath the soil, peek their heads out, and rise from the fertile green ground.

The fairies bring with them all the colorful energies that have lay dormant throughout the winter months. Beautiful streams of every color float from their wings as they rise and paint the flowers and the surroundings. Playful and happy, the faeries flutter about spreading the colors. You sit in awe to witness this beauty of the return of color and playful energies.

The fairies, one by one, come out of the earth and bring the promise of spring to the forest. The colors transform the feel in the air and your energy feels alive with hope and wonder.

Flying over the grass and mossy ground, the faeries bring each flower to bud. They carry up the pinks and yellows, purples and blues. Rising higher now, they fly through the trees and create leaf buds on their branches and color robins' eggs turquoise blue in their nests.

They fly the energies all the way to the sun, sparking a more brilliant yellow light to shine downward.

And soon, the faeries fly to surround you. You breathe in and embrace the energies of renewal they carry. With each breath in, you are opening to the promises of spring.

You can feel the awakening, the renewal, the rebirth in your breath. The colorful energies awaken you to feelings of aliveness, playfulness, and joy. Spring emerges within you and releases you, finally, from any last bit of winter's darkness.

With this release, your energy expands, stirring rejuvenation and revitalization rising from within you. Whatever seeds of intentions you planted in the earth are now being delivered to you by the faeries.

So think ... what good is returning?

What is being renewed?

What new is blooming for you with the arrival of spring?

See and feel the energies of it all those things taking form and shape before your eyes, filling your forest with promise. How does it feel to transition into a new picture of life?

With this new vision and promise, delicate yet strong wings sprout from your back—a pair of multicolored wings! As the faeries flutter playfully around you, they invite you to join them, so you take flight.

You fly with them throughout the forest just like the faeries, making a trail of brilliant colors and spreading your new energy. You watch in amazement as this beauty unfolds.

You have shifted from that winter stillness into any energy of action, play and aliveness. An energy of celebration, and all of your being feels alive!

You and the faeries flutter about and fly high into the sky. Colors streaming behind you create a beautiful rainbow that reaches high above your forest, perfectly arching in the bright blue sky. Playfully you slide down the rainbow, landing safely upon the mossy forest floor.

Journey's End Reward

Here at the rainbow's end, to your pot of gold. Gifts of spring all around you. Gifts of promise, hope, and renewal. With gratitude, you bid the faeries farewell and thank them for their presence and guidance during this journey.

Picking up the pot of gold, you make your way along the mossy trail taking in the all the renewed energy of spring.

Energetically, you bring back that promise and hope into this space and time. Feel yourself bit by bit coming back to the room.

Holding that energy gently in your lap, you bring it up to your heart, placing your hands on your heart and allowing all the positive energy, images, and promises from this journey to circulate throughout your body. The energy work has been done.

Coming fully back now.
Feeling wonderful in every way.
Feeling the promise of spring alive within you.

What wonders does this spring have in store for you?

_____

_____

_____

_____

Write an affirmation, a positive statement, you can say every day that declares you accept this good for yourself and others.

_____

_____

_____

_____

Hot Air Balloon

Freeing Ourselves, Cutting the Cords That Bind Us

Because we are energetic beings, we create energetic cords, or ties of attachment, to everything and everyone we encounter. Some of these cords are beautiful and healthy and bring us joy. Other cords are unhealthy, keep us back, and limit our ability to move forward freely. By cutting the unhealthy ties, we can more easily move into healing, reclaim our power, and free ourselves to experience new possibilities and wonders.

Packing Your Spiritual Backpack

What people, situations, and emotions in your life do you believe are keeping you down?

_____

_____

_____

_____

How would it feel to be free from them?

_____

_____

_____

_____

Setting Out
Relaxation

Breathe slowly and softly.
Gently close your eyes.
Settle in and make yourself very comfortable.
Breathe and just be,
preparing now for a beautiful journey within.

Let the outside world slowly slip away.
Let your body go loose and limp.
Feel lighter as you just let go.

Your breath becomes easy and slow.
Your awareness is on what is happening right here and now.
As you breathe, a warmth grows within and gently releases you
from any and all tension and stress.

Loosen any grip in your body,
your shoulders, your jaw, your abdomen.
Let go of any control.
Feel any stress, any strain, any weight you carry fall from your
shoulders
and down your back and be released to the ground.

With your breath, gather it all up and let it
now drop down to the ground like heavy weights …
and let it go … down, down to earth … let it all go.

Feel any heaviness in your chest, and breathe it all down into your hands, and drop it now like boulders falling to the ground.

Letting it all go.
Feeling lighter now.
Becoming still and quiet.
Flowing with the easy in and out of your breath.

A soft, calming energy runs through you,
easing your mind and easing your emotions.

From the top of your head to the tips of your toes, you are at peace.
Dwelling deeper and deeper within …

Journey

Imagine yourself walking in a vast open field. A beautiful, open setting where the green grass rolls for miles under your feet and a big sky stretches out as far as the eye can see. Here, there is an energy of expansiveness, of freedom, of peace and possibility. As you walk, you connect with this energy, breathe it in, and become part of it. Here, you feel safe and at ease.

Taking in clean air, your mind clears.
Breathing in peace, you feel free.

You hike to the top of a small hill and look out over the land. To your pleasant surprise, many hot air balloons are being released on the ground and floating through the unending blue sky.

What a glorious sight you have stumbled upon. You watch as these enormous balloons glide effortlessly through the vast blue sky, filling it with vibrant colors. They give out a carefree feeling of freedom and weightlessness, something you so desire to be part of and experience.

You run down the hill to where the balloons are being released and are delighted to find one last balloon that has not yet taken flight. You stand and notice its grandeur, all its colors and designs. It is perfect as if it was made just for you.

You are excited to take a journey upward in the balloon with the others and feel that freedom.

As you walk closer, you notice the balloon is fastened very tightly to the ground.

It is being held down by ropes and chains, attached very tightly to heavy boulders, keeping it from flying free like the others. So much weight. So much in the way to take flight.

You reflect on how these boulders keeping it grounded are very much like the things that hold you down. Things that keep you from your highest good and feeling free, that prevent you from soaring. Things that keep you from incredible possibilities, from new opportunities. You can see the connection now between you and the balloon's inability to fly, and you are determined to make a change.

At closer look, you notice there are words written on each boulder. Each word describes something that weighs you down. You walk around the balloon and read the words.

With the balloon securely fastened to the ground, you climb into its basket and search for something in which to cut the ropes and break the chains. You find the perfect tool, climb out of the basket, and begin cutting.

One by one, you cut and release yourself from that which binds you. Reading the words as you cut, releasing yourself as you release this balloon. Setting yourself free and getting yourself set up to soar!

With this done, you notice how you feel.

Quickly you climb back into the basket, ready to now take flight.

You launch the balloon and slowly rise into the air. Up into the vast blue sky, higher and higher you soar. Being carried by gentle winds, you feel safe floating upward, drifting with ease.

You watch the boulders below become smaller and smaller as you ascend higher into the tranquil sky. Here, a blissful silence and peace comes over you, a feeling of freedom. You have cut the chains and ropes that bind you, and you have released yourself to a higher good and great possibilities.

As you safely float, you pass above beautiful sights; the land below is like none you have ever seen. A whole new world has opened to you where there seems to be no end to the land. You notice familiar things below. Your town, your home, your world.

Familiar, yes, but different.

All of your world below is shimmering, changing and taking on a higher form right before your eyes. By releasing yourself from the boulders that bound you, your world is now different. It exists in a higher vibration built from the courage and determination of letting go, releasing those things that held you back and allowing yourself to be free.

When you land, you will not be returning the same as you were, nor will you be returning to the same world.

Your new world will match your new vibrations of feeling lighter and will hold greater possibilities now that you have set yourself free. Slowly and gently, you begin your descent to the ground, trusting the soft breeze to carry you carefully to the earth. Landing safely, you climb out of the basket and feel your feet touch the ground. When you're firmly planted in the earth, the energies of protection and guidance rise up from the ground and fill you.

Journey's End Reward

You are safe.
You look to the balloon and give thanks for all this journey has revealed.
You are ready to take soar and open to new possibilities, opportunities, and experiences.

Breathe in freedom.
And when you are ready,
slowly come back into the room, keeping your eyes closed.
Bringing back with you all the positive and empowering energy of this journey.
Bring your hands up to your heart, putting this energy into your heart.

And giving thanks to yourself for your courage.
Go in peace and soar.

What were the words on the boulders, and what do they describe?

_____

_____

_____

_____

What was the tool you used to cut the ropes and chains? Does it symbolize anything for you?

_____

_____

_____

_____

Describe how it felt to first take flight. How did it feel to be in flight?

_____

_____

_____

_____

What will change for the better by removing the weight and cutting what binds you?

_____

_____

_____

_____

Draw your balloon. Does its design have any significance for you?

Lotus Flower

From Suffering Comes Beauty

From suffering comes beauty. Within every challenging situation, there is a promise of rebirth, growing something beautiful, and gaining wisdom and enlightenment. The lotus, one of the most beautiful flowers, will grow only in mud. In this journey, you will explore your mud, your challenges, and the beauty it will bring into bloom.

Packing Your Spiritual Backpack

What is mud (situations and challenges) in which you have been standing?

_____

_____

_____

_____

What currently is keeping you from feeling empowered?

_____

_____

_____

_____

What promise and hope do you wish to come out of these experience?

_____

_____

_____

_____

Setting Out
Relaxation

Allow your eyes to gently close as
your breath eases you into relaxation.
Follow the soft in and out
and settle in deep to the ebb and flow of each breath.

Feel your breath flow over you,
warm you.
Let it release you into calm and stillness.
See the air you breathe as light,
feeling this light enter your lungs and fill your entire being.
It soothes you,
brings healing, and rejuvenates every cell, mind, body, and spirit.

Let the tender light take you inward.
Away from the outside world.
Transforming your vibration
into a rhythm of peace.

Let the light be your guide.
See it in front of you, unfolding outward and
spreading like a path under your feet.
Step onto this path of light and feels its shimmer run through you.

Experience yourself glimmer as millions of tiny speckles of light
sparkle all throughout your body.
Breathe
and let this light comfort you,

bringing you into peace and stillness
as you journey inward and forward.

Journey

You follow along the light, one step at a time. Confidently walking and trusting the light to lead you into an inner discovery filled with hope and promise.

Along this glistening path, you come to a mystical land filled with wonders and natural beauty. Amid the most breathtaking nature, lush green vegetation and large flowers grow in abundance.

Above, the sun peeks through a large canopy of trees, and a refreshing waterfall cascades down moss-covered rocks, making the air cool and misty. This land can be anything you wish, so make it as beautiful, as peaceful, and as magical as you desire.

Journeying forward with the path of light as your guide, you are le to a clearing, where you find a shallow pool of clean, clear water.

You walk to the edge of the pool and sit down to rest. Gazing into the water, you notice how clearly you can see your reflection. You run your fingers through the cool and inviting water and decide to remove your shoes to cool your feet.

The comfort of the water eases any tension in your feet and ankles, and the soft earth at the bottom of the pool invites you to dig in your toes and pull up its nurturing energy. As you stand in this pool, you connect with that life force that runs within you and feel rejuvenated.

Reaching down into the pool, you cup your hands, gather some water, and lift your hands to your head. Feel the refreshing water drip down your scalp. You continue to gather the water in your hands, pouring it over your head again and again.

It drips down your face, neck, and shoulders. Healing energies of this water release you from any stress and tension. All of the stress and tension and negativity you hold drip down with the water and empty into the pool. You are aware of what you are releasing.

The things you hold from challenges and disappointments immediately cascade down your body and into the water and leave you feeling lighter and renewed. Your whole being feels as clean and clear as the water in which you stand.

You breathe in relief, knowing any and all negativity you took on from life's challenges has released itself and washed away into the pool.

Looking down to your feet, you see the water in the pool has become murky and dark brown in color, the muddy, unappealing water created by all the negativity you have released. This is the mud of your pain, your challenges, your suffering, your stress and strain.

You stand in the ankle-high water and reflect on the mud you have encountered in your challenges and how holding on to for so long. You give thanks in its release.

While you reflect, the strangest thing begins to occur … Tiny green stems peek their way out of the mud and grow upward toward the sun. Hundreds upon hundreds of little green stems fill the pool.

They begin to sprout flower buds that hold the promise and hope of something beautiful. They hold the flower of the mystical lotus, the promise of empowerment and light.

As the sunlight bathes each bud, they suddenly burst into bloom, revealing to you their beauty and filling the air with an incredible soothing fragrance.

You stand in amazement as the entire pool is brimming with lotus in full bloom and are intrigued how something so delicate and beautiful could rise from such dirty, murky, and muddy water.

You take a moment to think about the beauty that is promised from your own life's mud, from your challenges, situations, heartbreak, and disappointment. You reflect on how you will be empowered having had these experiences, and you can feel a sense of greater understanding stir within you.

A soft, hazy mist of light begins to flow from the center of each lotus. You watch the mist float up and fill the air with a soft, glimmering light. You wave your hands through the mist and can feel it shimmer on your skin.

The mist embraces you, wrapping you sweetly in a cocoon of its shimmering softness. It touches your heart and spreads all throughout your being. From this you come to understand that out of the mud, beauty is birthed, and you reflect on what is to bloom out of your personal mud.

Without the mud, there can be no lotus.
Without the challenges and pain, there can be no beauty.

The mist of the lotus swirls and shimmers around you, purifying and transforming your mind and body. It brings to you a state of clear mind and health. And you stand in this pool, blooming as beautifully as the lotus flowers, restored, enlightened, and with new understanding.

All of the mud you've experienced has had purpose. It has brought you to this place and time and has birthed a promise of abundant beauty in your life.

Journey's End Reward

You give thanks to the mud, the water, and the flowers for the healing, and you hope it has revealed to you and carefully step out of the pool, shimmering and shining like the mist.

You pick one flower as a symbol of what is promised and once again step onto the path of light. You follow the light, but this time in a different direction, taking you a different way home through the mystical forest. You now walk on a path of greater light, a path lit by your own enlightenment, illuminated with new hope and promise.

Stay in this feeling as you walk yourself back into this room.
Entering back into the present moment.
Feeling renewed and relaxed.
Breathe in the energy of this journey.
Take that energy into your lungs and feel the difference in the flow of your energy …
Lighter, cleaner, clearer.

And when you are ready, slowly feel your body back in here and now.

Gently open your eyes and return refreshed.

How did it feel to wash away the negative energy of you challenges?

_____

_____

_____

_____

What beauty is blooming out of your mud? What beauty is blooming from your suffering?

_____

_____

_____

_____

What else was revealed to you during this journey?

_____

_____

_____

_____

Rolling Waves

Trust, Surrender, Courage

Healing can truly begin when we find the courage to surrender to trust and let things just be. In all challenges, there comes a moment where we have decided we have struggled enough and realize there is nothing more to do but trust.

Packing Your Spiritual Backpack

What are you experiencing that you are doing everything you can to make better?

_____

_____

_____

_____

If you could trust and let it be, how would you experience the situation differently?

_____

_____

_____

_____

Setting Out
Relaxation

Close your eyes and
breathe in very slowly.
Hold and now breathe out.
Take a few more breaths
and feel yourself begin to let go.

With each exhale, you are letting go physically.
Any tension or strain fades away through your breath.
Any heaviness you may be carrying easily releases itself.
Bring your breath to wherever tension has settled in your body.
Gather it all up and breathe it into your lungs, and with one huge
breath, forcefully let it all go.

Let it all just leave,
freeing your body and leaving your mind.
Exhale it all out into nothingness.
Surrender all control
and watch as it just floats further and further away.

Let go of the grip you have on what is happening in your life.
Whatever this is, you can feel safe in letting it go.

So be gentle with yourself.
Give yourself permission to surrender now to peace,
to experience the natural flow of your breath without the stress
and strain.
Just let the life force flow

and with each new breath in … just be.

Soften your being and sink deep into where you are.
You can begin to trust you are nurtured, loved, and supported in this and every moment.

Surrender to the soothing sense of comfort within and slip deeply into this trust as a flow of peace carries you to gently forward.

Journey

Imagine yourself walking along a pristine, white sandy beach, enjoying the soft sand under your toes. You listen to the sound of the gentle waves lapping onto shore and journey peacefully along the water's edge. A warm breeze blows through the palm trees that line shore.

With each step in the sand, you feel more calm and more at ease. As you walk, you reflect on all the good life has brought you and count your blessings.

You think about any challenges you are facing and how hard you work to make your way through them. You think about where you try to control the situations and wonder how it would feel if you could loosen your grip, even just a little bit, and trust everything will be okay.

The water of the sea is inviting and warm, and you decide to take a little swim. You wade into the water and feel it soothe your body. Swimming out a little distance from shore, you make sure to go just far enough to feel completely safe. The beach looks beautiful from out in the water. The sand glistens in the sun, and the palm trees gently sway in the breeze while you swim.

Here in the crystal clear blue-green water, you take time to rest and float effortlessly on your back and relax.

Feeling very safe.

The sun above warms your face, and the support of the salty sea beneath you holds you up. You cherish this well-deserved rest beneath the blue sky while you watch the wispy white clouds drift by here and there in the sky. You are safe and so at peace …

Soothed by the gentle rolling of waves beneath you, you feel weightless and free. It is easy to surrender to the peace and allow yourself to be in this moment and just rest. There is nothing for you to do and nowhere for you to be, so you relax. The rhythmic waves softly rock you as you float and lull you into a place of blissful peace. All is very well.

After some time, you notice the sky is beginning to change. Many clouds move in and thicken, turning from a clean white to dusty gray. The pleasant breeze becomes a bit stronger, and the once gentle rolling of the waves is slightly rougher.

You stop floating and decide you need to swim back to shore. The waves grow bigger and bigger, and the current becomes stronger. Determined, you swim forward, struggling as you make your way.

Almost in an instant, the sea becomes very rough. The waves reach higher and come more frequently.

It takes all you have to make it through this rougher water, fighting against the large waves and fast current.

You fight and struggle as you swim harder, trying everything you can to get back to shore. Yet no matter how you try, you make very little progress forward. With each wave, the struggle gets more difficult, and at times you seem to be going backward and farther out to sea. Noticing the land getting smaller and farther away, your fight appears hopeless at times.

Within all this struggle, a single ray of sunlight shines down from an otherwise gray sky. This single ray of light shines directly on you, bringing to you warmth and sense of hope. This light beckons you to do one thing: stop! It asks you to release the struggle, let go of the control, and just let it just be.

The warmth of this light shines like a beacon, bringing you hope and releasing a courage within you, helping you to trust and let go of the struggle

You catch your breath as the waves around you continue to roll rapidly beneath you. Returning to floating on your back, you decide to trust what you feel in the warmth of that ray of light. Slowly you let go, trust, and become more still, slowly releasing the fight and surrendering your body to just float.

The ray of light stays with you as the waves carry you forward. In your surrender, the waves seem to roll with more rhythm and seem to get a little smaller. The tide appears to shift, and you realize you are being carried on the waves back to shore.

The sea is far from calm, but you roll with the waves without resistance and with a greater sense of assurance. Your breathing returns to normal as the waves carry you, and your body relaxes and lets go. You allow everything around you to just be as it is, and before long, safely you find yourself back onto the white sandy shore.

Upon reaching the beach safely, you walk out of the water and on to the dry sand. You turn to watch as some of the dark clouds disperse and drift out to sea. The sun shines a little more brightly, and its rays reach out to warm your face. Each ray that makes its way through the leftover clouds touches your skin nurtures and greets you with warm, unconditional love.

In your surrender, in the letting go of the struggle, you have come to a place of trust. You have released the control and reclaim your sense of peace, letting it all be and knowing it'll all be okay.

A soft wind now whirls around you, welcoming you back. It carries a sense of comfort in its sweet embrace.

Turning to look at the sea, you notice the rough waters are still in sight yet slowly calming.

Journey's End Reward

In surrendering to trust, you understand that there are times when the waves will curl up and the clouds will sometimes go dark. It is safe to release control and roll with the tide. You will be safely brought out of the challenge, and the sun will come to shine bright again. The most important thing to do is trust.

So quietly bring yourself back to this moment in time.
Feeling that great courage you possess.

Feeling lighter from having relinquished control.
Bring back that newly found sense of inner peace.
And bring with you a new trust in life, no matter what happens.

Breathe.
Open your eyes.
Sense the space around you.
Feel pride in your courage throughout this journey and going forward.

What were you feeling when the sea became rough?

_____

_____

_____

_____

What, if anything, did the ray of light symbolize?

_____

_____

_____

_____

What did you learn about yourself throughout this journey?

_____

_____

_____

_____

What can you start doing right now to help you trust and surrender?

_____

_____

_____

_____

You Are a Beacon of Light and Hope

We have all weathered many personal storms. During those times, certain people, or perhaps certain things, have been like lighthouses, our own personal beacons of hope. Because of them, we gather strength to endure even the most difficult of times and come out the other side, a lighthouse for someone else.

What personal storms have you recently survived?

_____

_____

_____

_____

Was there anyone in particular that helped you? In what way were others a beacon of light and hope?

_____

_____

_____

_____

Setting Out
Relaxation

Become soft and gentle where you are …
Feel the weight of the day and week just fall away.
Allow a warm light to cascade down from the top of your head,
into your eyes, cheeks, and jaw, releasing you from any stress and
strain.

Feel all your muscles loosen and let go,
and your shoulders now go limp.
Your upper and lower back now relaxes, and all the muscles of
your hips and legs let go.

Let yourself fall deep into comfort
Feeling lighter as you breathe.
Lighter and lighter.
A sense of freedom comes over you.
You become as light as a feather now.

Imagine you are drifting on a gentle breeze,
safely drifting inward as the world just fades away.

Feel yourself drift into a blissful and peaceful state.

Journey

Drifting downward through the sky … and landing softly atop a
sandy white dune by the shore. Here, you lie peacefully on your

back, looking up the sky. The sand beneath your body is supportive and warm. The nurturing sun shines down, replenishing your entire being with light. Lying in a tranquil and soothing setting, you are grateful for this time to just be.

You stand and look out over the dune. Tall sea grass grows to either side of you, and beyond the grass, a blue-green sea is shining.

Barefoot in the sand, you sink your feet in deep and absorb the soft comfort. The Earth's nurturing energies rise up and enter through the bottom of your feet. All is well and as it should be …

It is nearly summer's end, where the days have become more quiet and less busy. It is a nostalgic time. The passing of summer draws you into reflection and gratitude for all it brought.

Here on a sandy path along the dune, you can see the water stretching out far and wide to either side of you. In this moment, you inhale the serenity and treasure this time just for you.

You brush your fingertips along the tall sea grass as you walk the sandy path. The fragrance of sea roses greets you as you pass each bush abundant with blossoms. The gulls call out from over head, acknowledging your presence to one another. You breathe and take in the clean and salty air.

This path soon opens to a long thin beach that stretches out into the water like a peninsula. In the distance, a lighthouse stands tall, strong and still. You set out to follow the narrow beach that leads to the lighthouse, listening to the calm waters lapping very quietly onto shore.

Seashells and unique rocks sparkle on the beach, and boats sail off into the blue green horizon. It is a serene and peaceful day

On your approach to the lighthouse, you come upon a peculiar sight. Stacks and stacks of stones cover the beach as far as the eye can see. The stones have been purposely placed one on top of the other, creating very unique and special structures. Some stacks are very large, some are quite small, yet each is artistic and unique in its own way.

You have seen stacks like these before and know they are markings made to commemorate something special or honor a sacred space.

You gingerly walk around the stones, showing respect and honoring the people who built them and the special reasons why. Reflecting on each stone stack, you quietly take a moment to remember what made this summer memorable. You reminisce about all the special moments, fondly recalling all the happy times and the laughter of friends and family. Perhaps there were trip taken and goals accomplished that made this summer ever more memorable.

You give thanks for what the summer brought to you and continue on your way to the lighthouse. Carefully passing through the stone garden, you come to the base of lighthouse and look up.

Standing tall and built of stone itself, the lighthouse exudes an aura of strength and endurance. Reaching out, you run your hands along the stone side of the lighthouse. It feels smooth, weathered, and worn from decades, maybe centuries, of many storms. Yet here it still stands, tall and strong, a beacon of light and comfort for so many over the years.

You reflect for a moment on the many storms you have experienced and survived, and you can't help but feel an immediate connection to the lighthouse.

Making your way around to the front, you find an opening. You push open a very heavy door that leads you into a short hallway. A wrought-iron spiral staircase at your feet curves upward to the top. With excitement you lift your foot onto the first step and slowly ascend, one step at a time.

As you climb, you think of the lighthouse keepers that once lived here over the years. You reflect on what an important job they had, keeping the light burning as a beacon of hope and safety to so many over the years, never actually knowing whom it helped and why.

As you round each curve of the stairs, you pass windows that give you different views of the sea and notice the slowly setting sun in the sky. You run your hands along the cool, sturdy stone walls all the way to the top.

At the top, a small ladder leads you to where the lighthouse lens sits. You marvel at how it turns and shines its light outward, and how this one light can reach so many people as it shines far out and over the water.

A circular perch surrounds the top of lighthouse. You step outside to enjoy the view of the early evening sky radiating beautiful hues of pinks, oranges, and reds. Slowly the sky puts the day to bed and gives rise to the dark night.

The light stretching out appears brighter in the darker sky and changes your perceptive. It circles about, reaching out and making visible sailboats and other vessels off in the far distance.

The light brings comfort to the tiny vessels at sea as it swings around again and again, assuring those on their journeys through the dark night that they will be provided with safe passage home.

You stand still, strong, and tall upon this perch and feel a deep connection with the lighthouse. You reflect on the many moments when you have had to be strong for others and how you too sent out an inner light in reassurance.

Suddenly, you realize what the lighthouse is here to teach. You remember having been a shining light and a beacon of hope and refuge for others, and now you see the similarities between you and this lighthouse.

Here on the perch, you stand still and stretch out your arms over the sea, feeling your inner light growing and glowing. You send it out, radiating over the water just like the light from the lighthouse.

As your light stretches out far and wide, you think of those you love, imagining your light reaching and greeting them with a warm embrace. You send your light out to any and all in need, not ever knowing who you will reach and the hope you may bring to them or why. You imagine your light reaches out to many distant shores and illuminates anyone who is need of hope, refuge, and a sense of comfort.

This brings to mind the many times and situations when someone close to you, or maybe even a stranger, was a beacon of light for you, and now in turn, you are being one for someone else.

Like the lighthouse, you may never truly know who you are helping, but you stand tall for them anyway, give out your light, and let it empower who it will and lift them to a place of hope.

Someday, they too will stand tall and strong and be a beacon of hope for someone else. You hold tight to this and know the time has come for you to leave.

You start down the curvy stairs, pass the windows, and head out the heavy door. You walk to the front of the lighthouse, the farthest-most point on the peninsula, and look out over the sea.

Journey's End Reward

Gathering up some stones from the ground, some small and some large, you make a pile and think about all you have learned from this journey. With your stones, you build a stack, carefully placing one on top of the other.

Let this stack represent this moment in time and be a marker of the wisdom and knowledge you have gathered here. This special place has been a beacon of light and hope in your own healing, giving you strength to weather your personal storms.

Go in peace to shine your light, be a bright beacon of light, and bring hope and comfort to others in need.

Breathe and once again feel yourself slowly begin to drift upward, feeling like a feather, light and airy. Let the soft breeze whisk you into the night sky and bring you safely floating back.

Coming back to this space and time.
Coming back to this room, peaceful and quiet.
Feeling your inner light strong and confidently go forward in peace.

Describe any connection you may feel with the lighthouse.

_____

_____

_____

_____

What did your stack of stones symbolize for you?

_____

_____

_____

_____

How can you begin today to be a beacon of hope for someone else?

_____

_____

_____

_____

Sanctuary of Stillness

Stillness, Wisdom, Connecting with Source

We have all experienced challenging times when nothing seems to slow down or get any better. Often this abundance of activity leads us to lose sight of our light and our source. We lose our focus and often forget to ground ourselves in order to stay centered and levelheaded while we wait for the situation to calm down.

Our vision can become distorted by all the movement, emotion, and activity. However, in practicing stillness, we are better able to experience the full view and gain wisdom. Stillness allows us to continue on with what we are going through without losing sight of the light. Stillness allows us the opportunity to ground ourselves to better handle the challenging chaotic energy.

Preparing Your Spiritual Backpack

Describe any difficult movement or activity in your life.

_____

_____

_____

_____

What influence does this activity have on you emotionally and physically?

Experiencing certain activity can feel many different ways at the same time.

Describe all the ways the activity in your life feels (e.g., chaotic, productive, hurried, useful, worrisome, heartbreaking).

_____

_____

_____

_____

Setting Out
Relaxation

Feel your body where you sit or lie.
Breathe in deep and allow each part of you to suddenly soften.
Breathing away the day, the week, the month,
just letting the physical world fall away.

Allow your eyes to gently close naturally.
Begin to settle in deep where you are.
Surrender now to the idea of being still, quiet, and at peace.
Put your attention on your mind and
breathe away any thoughts, watching them gently break apart and
float far, far away.
Create as best you can a clear, empty space in your mind,
allowing it to settle into stillness and peace.

Feel the smooth softness of your breath going in and out.
And allow yourself to slip further and further inward …

From your feet, imagine strong, thick roots growing deep down
into the soil of Mother Earth.
Let them take gentle hold in her nurturing ground and root you
in safety and security.
At all times, know you are safe.
The earth gently holds you, no matter where you are or whatever
you are experiencing.
Feel that safe, warm, motherly hold rise from the earth and into
your feet and legs.

This warm, loving energy travels up your hips, back, and torso.
It sweetly holds your entire body as it moves up to your head.
Your entire being is now grounded in the loving earth,
giving you the freedom to slip into a deep blissful and healing
space.

Your breath grows calmer and calmer,
your body still and relaxed.
And you are ready to embrace this soothing, soft stillness and
just be …

Journey

Imagine yourself resting comfortably on the ground, deep within
the woods. You lie on your back and feel the soft, cool moss
beneath your body.

Your face is pointed to the sky, where the sun beams downward
through the heavy canopy of tree and warms your face. Let this
place become a sanctuary where you have to come to rest and
rejuvenate.

The trees around you have grown naturally in a circle. Lush with
leaves, they shade where you are and allow the moss to grow like
carpet beneath your body. Your hands reach out to feel the velvet
softness of the moss, cool and comfortable to the touch.

Here, all is calm and serene. Resting is a welcome and well-
deserved change from the chaos and activity of life.

You lie still on this beautiful day in sacred space and take a few
deep breaths. The air has a clean, fresh, crisp energy that fills the

woods. Besides the occasional the sound of the birds, there is a pleasant silence.

Your entire being rests, soaking in renewal and healing from the pure, untouched energy of the woods. You can feel this energy running through you as you breathe, bringing healing to every cell and allowing you time to be still.

You look up at the circles of trees and see they too exist in a quiet stillness. One tree stands out among the rest. It has grown strong and tall and exists in a quiet grace.

Your eyes go to its roots. Roots that have firmly grabbed onto Mother Earth and grown large and wide above and beneath her soil. Roots that have created a secure and supportive home for the tree, remind you of any support and security you too have created in your life.

You rest, firmly planting yourself in Mother Earth, and lie quiet and still. You imagine roots like the tree's growing out from under you and into the rich, nurturing soil.

Your vision follows the tree roots slowly up to her trunk, and you take notice of her bark, mature and detailed. As you examine her bark, you notice patterns of dark and light, smooth areas and cracks as well.

Her bark tells the story of her life. From infancy and childhood, then into adolescence and adulthood, this tree bark tells a story … and not one very different from your own.

It has grown, like you, through the many happy sunny days and many wild storms. This tree, like you, has a story to be told.

Your eyes follow the line of the trunk and bark as it branches off in many directions.

Each branch takes a different journey and reminds you of your own many branches in life.

You too have taken many journeys and branched out in many different ways. Some happy and some challenging, yet all the time, you, like the tree, were rooted in the safety and security of the Earth.

Some branches were journeys with your friends, some with your family, and still some branches are journeys you traveled completely alone.

You notice that some branches have grown as far as they can, whereas others are still growing. This reminds you of the journeys that are finished and the others you are still traveling.

Green leaves have grown on every branch. Green, the color of love, fills your tree. And like your own life, so many leaves of love have grown out of the branches of your life.

Love, in some way, has come to grow out of every branch. Reflecting on even the most difficult times, you recall the love that came from each one.

You lie still on the ground, absorb the green of the leaves, and hold that love in your heart. Remembering, you give thanks for each and every branch and the love they sprouted.

Your eyes follow the tree further upward as it reaches into the sky. It extends gracefully and with strength toward the sun, and its very top seems to disappear into the light. The tree reaches outward and upward to the sun, appearing to transform into light itself. Here, it connects with its source of life force energy, its source of nourishment, of comfort and healing.

The tree connects with its source at its top, its crown like you. You take a moment to remember this and point your face to the sun filtering through the trees to reconnect.

You are nourished by the sun's rays beaming warmly downward and soak it all in. The light is so comforting as it connects with you and touches your crown, your face, your chest. You welcome that soft light and bathe fully in it as you rejuvenate and heal.

Ever reaching upward toward its source, this tree has survived and healed from every storm. It has grown and thrived pointing itself all the time to its true source for guidance and nourishment.

A gentle breeze begins to blow, making every tree around the circle sway ever so slightly. Back and forth, gracefully and gently, they rock in the breeze. As they sway, the sun goes in and out, sometimes putting you in shade, sometimes shining brightly upon you. You take notice of how the movement in the trees appears to make the light disappear.

Soon the wind picks up again. More powerful than before, this wind creates a great sway in the trees, a disruption to their peaceful stillness.

You watch the forceful bending of the trees toward the ground and admire how they stay rooted in the soil throughout all this turbulence. They do not fight the wind; instead, they gracefully let it take its course. At times, the winds blows so strong, you think the trees will surely break and be knocked down to the ground. Yet they remain rooted to the earth and wait in strength for the challenging wind to pass.

From your perspective, you can see the light of the sun stays constant even when the wind blows its strongest. In your stillness, you observe how it only appears to go in and out as the trees sways. It even seems to disappear at times. Yet you can now see it is always present, despite the movement in the chaotic wind.

Eventually, the wind dies down, and the trees once again stand tall and still. In their stillness, they seem to regroup themselves, returning to pointing their tops upward and face the light. They do this so naturally and with such trust, knowing all along the light never left.

Journey's End Reward

In our busiest moments, in our most challenges times, it is important to remember our source, our light, only seems to disappear. Our vision tends to be distorted by our own winds in life, making the light appear to go in and out and sometimes not be there at all. Yet from a place of stillness, we can see it remains a constant throughout any chaos. It is always guiding us, always present. Always there to reach for. Always a source of strength, guidance, and nourishment.

Only in our stillness can we recognize this and connect.

Continuing to lie quietly on the ground, you reflect on where there is movement in your life. You think about the ways in which have you lost connection with the source, the light, throughout this time. In your stillness, there is an opportunity to keep connected throughout any chaos you experience.

From the mossy ground, you get up and stand tall. You walk over to your tree and hold it in your arms, thanking it for anything it taught you today.

Before you leave this sanctuary of stillness, you can decide to bring with you the stillness you experienced. You can decide to allow yourself to experience the ever-present light, to remain focused and levelheaded by finding stillness when the winds blow wild.

So gently breathe your way back.
Slowly feel your body for head to toe.
Open your eyes. Take a nice breath.
And revel in the stillness for a few more minutes.

How did it feel to imagine yourself lying still?

_____

_____

_____

_____

What, if anything, did the bark of the tree reveal to you?

_____

_____

_____

_____

Describe your branches and the journeys in your life they represented.

_____

_____

_____

_____

Where can you start to insert the practice of stillness in your daily life?

_____

_____

_____

_____

What are your sources of spiritual and emotional nourishment?

_____

_____

_____

_____

Loosening the Blanket of Security

Trusting Self, Letting Go

During our darkest times, we often tend to create a "security blanket" in order to soothe ourselves and feel safer. This security blanket can be any object that makes us feel safe and hopeful, and at times it can even include people. As we transition from difficult to easier times, we often keep a tight hold on our security blanket. We continue to believe we still need it to feel safe. Only when we loosen our grip, and even let the security blanket go completely, can we grow to trust and have faith in ourselves.

Packing your Spiritual Backpack

What have you used in the past as a security blanket (what object or person) to soothe and comfort you during a difficult time?

_____

_____

_____

_____

In what way do you continue to use this object or person as a security blanket?

_____

_____

_____

_____

What changes in yourself would you see and feel if you loosened your grip or completely let it go?

_____

_____

_____

_____

Setting Out
Relaxation

Place your hands on your belly.
Slowly breathe, in and out, softly and naturally.
Feel your hands rise and fall with your breath.
Let this be comforting and soothing.

The soft sound of your breath brings you inward
and lulls you into a pleasant state of relaxation.
The rhythm of your breath calms you,
releases you from the world without, and brings you deep into a
blissful haven within.

Let this gentle rhythm guide you,
flowing up into your head, clearing your mind.
Let it roll over your body and release you of any weight you carry,
any stress or strain.
Completely releasing you.
Let your breath
soothe your soul and put you at ease.

You are calm.
You are still.
You now let go …
gently drifting inward with the rhythm of your breath.

Journey

Imagine it is late autumn, just before dawn. You find yourself sleeping on a mountaintop, where the sky is still a bit dark and the air is fresh and cool.

Here, you lie on soft dirt overlooking a cliff. Here, you have found comfort to take rest after traveling a long journey up the difficult mountain trail.

Breathing in the fresh air, you wake to the breaking of dawn. Wrapped in a heavy old blanket, you were held in security and safety through the dark night. This blanket soothed you when feeling alone and scared. It gave you reassurance and a sense of protection.

You wake to witness the chilly, dark night leaving. All is still and quiet. The only movement is that of the sky transforming as the night slowly slips out of view.

There is much meaning in the transformation from night to day. You welcome the long-awaited new light and reflect on what you yourself are emerging from, reflect on any darkness and difficult times.

As the sun arrives, it transforms the earth from its dark, cold stillness into joyful light.

Soft colors of yellows, pinks, and oranges stream out from behind the mountains. This transformation quietly unfolds, bringing into view other mountains in the distance. You know those mountains because you have successfully climbed them in the past.

The sun's first rays stream outward, bringing you a sense of hope. You loosen your blanket a little around your chest and shoulders, welcoming in the light.

As the rays touch your chest, they fill your heart with a renewed faith in yourself. Just like night turning to day, you can feel a transformation occurring within.

Looking down at your blanket, you now notice you feel a bit too warm beneath its embrace. This blanket has had purpose and has been a symbol of anything that has brought you a sense of safety and comfort. You reflect on your life and anything that has served you as a security blanket during difficult times.

Whatever it is, it is now time to loving and gratefully let it go. With the dark times out of view, you can begin again to feel safe on your own, trust yourself, and declare you are now ready to go forward.

You can decide to let the blanket go and be free. And so you stand, and slowly you unravel yourself from its hold. You loosen the blanket a bit more from your shoulders and chest, thanking it for how it has been of service, sheltering you through all the difficult times, through pain, through sorrow, through disappointment.

You thank the blanket and, when you are ready, let it fall to the ground at your feet. This is a big step for you. You lovingly look down at your blanket—now a tired, old, worn-out blanket, something of security and symbol from a past journey.

You watch it disintegrate before your eyes, giving yourself permission to completely let it go. With it disintegrates any fear, any lack of faith, any self-doubt …

All gone, and you take notice how it feels to set yourself free.

The sun continues to rise in the early morning sky. The light is more intense now, and you can feel it filling you, transforming you, and bathing you in hope. You take time to reflect ……

From what are you transforming?

What were the journey and the challenges?

What effects did they have on you physically, emotionally, and spiritually?

Along your way, you may have taken on fear, negativity, and worry. But in this moment, any darkness, any heaviness can now fall away and be transformed with the rising light. A new sense of trust in yourself emerges. A new confidence begins to grow.

You begin to feel lighter and more alive. In letting go of anything that may have brought you a false sense of security, you have made room for the new. You have made room for the freedom to grow, to believe in yourself, to transform into a higher vibration of light, and to experience a new expression of yourself.

You take a deep breath and feel relieved. You stand, calm and at peace.

Overhead, a single bird flies and calls in celebration of your transformation. A feather falls from its body and lands in your hands. It is perfect, soft, and smooth to the touch.

On the feather, words appear: "I am now."
You read the words over and over again.

"I am now … I am now …"

You look to your feet where your blanket disintegrated, and using the point of the feather, you write these words.

"I am now …"

You finish the sentence by writing in the dirt …
I am now free.
I am now capable.
I am now brave.
I am now light.
I am now confident.
I am now transformed.
I am now free.

Stepping back, you read them, ingest them, and absorb them as truth. Trusting in yourself. Believing in yourself. Having a renewed faith in your abilities to go forward in grace and strength.

Journey's End Reward

The sun reaches its highest place in the sky, and you feel your own light emerge within. This is your light of confidence and self-assurance. Your light of self-trust and faith.

Bowing to the sun, you give thanks for its light and the inner transformation that has occurred. It has taken courage to shed those things that once brought you security, to let go of any fear. And you can feel proud. With renewed trust and faith in yourself, you can emerge each day to stand tall and feel safe in your own light.

You turn to find a path in the woods that will lead you down the mountain. Confidently, you follow the path back to the here and now. Feel your body as you return renewed and refreshed. Bringing back from this journey the confidence and strength.

Embraced in your own light.
Come back strong, alive, and feeling good and confident in every way.
When you are ready, open your eyes …

How did it feel to let go of the blanket?

_____

_____

_____

_____

In what ways can you begin to trust and rely on yourself to feel safe?

_____

_____

_____

_____

What words did you use to complete the sentence "I Am now …"?

I Am now … _____

I Am now … _____

I Am now … _____

Write a daily affirmation that can help you feel confident and have faith in yourself.

_____

_____

_____

_____

Along a Pebbly Beach

Going with the Flow, Everything is Temporary, Acceptance

There is a natural ebb and flow to everything in life. Good flows into our lives in abundance and brings us joy. However, difficult situations can flow as well, stay for a long time, and bring us pain.

And all things ebb. What we see as good will at times disappear or seem scarce in our lives, making us impatient and lose trust. Yet difficult times also ebb, leaving us to feel carefree and light and joyous.

No matter what is happening, inner peace can come only through acceptance. Trusting and having patience can help us feel peaceful through the natural ebbs and flows of life.

Packing Your Spiritual Backpack

What are the areas of your life where you are experiencing an ebb, a lack, or a recession? How do you feel about this ebb?

_____

_____

_____

_____

In what areas is there a flow, an abundance, good or bad? How does it make you feel?

_____

_____

_____

_____

Setting Out
Relaxation

So close your eyes and breathe naturally.
Bring your awareness to your breath.
Notice how easily it flows in and out.
How it happens so naturally that you trust your next breath will
always be there.

Feel the natural rise and fall of your chest.
Let your breath relax you as you continue to trust and be still.

Each breath in clears your mind and relaxes you.
Each breath out releases you from the outer world and gently
brings you within.

Breathe into the muscles of your face, your eyes, your jaw …
Feel the breath release you from any tension and stress.
Breathe a sense of calm into your head and neck and upper back.
With each breath, you settle in deeper
to a warm feeling of comfort.
Let your breath massage into your shoulders … releasing the
tension.
Just relax.

Journey

Find yourself walking among tall palm trees that line the shore
and sway in the gentle breeze. The very early evening sky is just

beginning to show signs of the setting sun. Orange and pink hues streak through the fading blue canvas, and another day is coming to an end.

From the palm trees, the soft sand leads you down to where a pebbly beach meets the incoming waves. The cooling sand feels comforting beneath your feet.

At the water's edge, the tide rolls in, tickling your toes with refreshment.

You stand and watch the waves advance and recede. There is a natural in and out.
There is a natural push and pull.

You simply take notice of the ebb and flow of the water and contemplate how this applies to your life at this given moment. Ebbs and flows occur naturally everywhere in life.

As the waves crest and come to shore, you ponder the flow in your life. What things, what people, what opportunities are coming to you in an abundance? As the waves recede, or ebb, you recall where something you once had is now dwindling or even missing from your life altogether. Where are you experiencing an ebb?

By watching the waves, you can come to understand that everything is temporary. What you experience in great abundance today can be washed away by the changing tide tomorrow. The opposite is true: anything lacking can be brought back to you in abundance with the changing day.

You stand in the sand on your shore of life. The water is a symbol of the ebbing and flowing through your journey.

You sink your feet deep into the sand and let the water anchor them into the shore. You ground yourself and bring up the energy of safety and security. No matter what is ebbing and no matter what is flowing, you can always feel safe on your journey.

You turn now to take a walk along the shore toward the setting sun. On the sand are pebbles, sea glass, and shells. You notice how they feel under your bare feet as you walk. Some are smooth and cooling; others are jagged and rough.

Each pebble, each shell, and each piece of sea glass represents something that has flowed onto your shore of life—things you may have asked for, and some you may have not.

Some of the pebbles, shells, and sea glass represent people, friends, and lovers. Others represent opportunities, wealth, or service. Some have flowed to your shore, bringing joy. Some have washed up, bringing pain.

You stand still, watching the waves roll in over and over again. They move the shells and pebbles as they ebb and flow. Sometimes there is an abundance at your feet, at other times the shells and pebbles are spread out far from each other along the sand, and sometimes there are no shells or beach glass at all.

With each roll of the wave, the dynamic of your shore changes, reminding you everything is temporary.

You search the shore for those things that represent what you are most grateful for, those things that bring you joy. You gather up sea glass, shells, and pebbles that have brought joy in abundance. Perhaps there are other objects you see like driftwood, feathers, and starfish. You decide what they represent for you, what good they symbolize. You give thanks for their presence in your life right now, enjoy them, and then place them back on the shoreline at your feet.

There are jagged pebbles, sharp sea glass, and the broken shells along your shore as well. These are things you may not have wanted to flow into your world, yet here they are here. You breathe and remember everything is temporary.

These unwanted things have flowed into your life and have not brought you joy. You notice them, thank them for what they are here to teach. In giving thanks, you let them go with love. Wait patiently, knowing the tide will change and the waves will move them and carry them away.

You take a minute to notice what is missing from your shoreline— what people, what things, what opportunities. Whatever is missing (or in scarcity), trust that it is okay. You look back to the waves and remember the natural ebb and flow of the water. The natural in and out the natural push and pull. Remembering to be patient, trusting that everything is temporary. Knowing whatever is missing, you can now begin to accept that one day, it will return.

Journey's End Reward

Because you know and trust everything is temporary, you have embraced the flow of good with gratitude and can learn to accept the presence of the unwanted with patience.

At the same time, you are aware of what is ebbing or lacking in your life, but by looking to the waves, you can take comfort that the flow will once again return.

Continuing to walk into the sunset, you realize this day is done. With all its blessings and perhaps disappointment, it was a temporary moment in time.

The light in the sky begins to dwindle as the night flows in as promised. The moon appears and shines brightly above. It illuminates your beach and creates a glimmer on the water. Each little pebble on the sand glistens. Each piece of sea glass sparkles.

You take comfort, now knowing for sure that once again the sun will rise and the tide will shift, and you can trust yourself to handle all that ebbs and flows.
All is as it should be.
All is at peace.

Begin to breathe yourself back to the present.
Bring this beautiful feeling back with you.
Pull it into your solar plexus.
Breathe it into every muscle and every cell.

Feel a balance run through your body,
and when you are ready …
come softly back to the here and now.

Go in blessings and love.

How can you begin to practice patience and trust?

_____

_____

_____

_____

What can you do each day to remind yourself that everything is only temporary?

_____

_____

_____

_____

What can you do differently while you wait for the tide in some areas of your life to change?

_____

_____

_____

_____

Into Fullness

Wholeness, Fulfillment

We all feel a yearning to feel full, to achieve the wholeness of who we are. Yet there will always be times when life's challenges and disappointments take us away from feeling whole and rob us of parts of ourselves. This journey explores being aware of where we feel complete, what is missing, and how to move forward into attaining what we need to help us feel as close to whole as possible.

Packing Your Spiritual Backpack

Take a moment to create an inventory of your life as it is right now. What is already adding to the feeling of being complete, full, and satisfied?

_____

_____

_____

_____

What is missing that would make you feel more complete?

_____

_____

_____

_____

How would you be different if you discovered and gave to yourself those things that are missing?

_____

_____

_____

_____

Setting Out
Relaxation

Quiet yourself and soften your breath.
Calm your body and clear your mind.
Sink into where you sit and let your breath fall into a natural,
soft rhythm.
The chaotic world around you now slips further and further away.
Your breath brings you within, quieting your thoughts.
Your thoughts are quiet.
You travel into that sacred space within,
that blissful, still place of peace.

Breathe yourself even deeper inward,
into the very core of your being
to that very central point of your light body within.

Let the light in the center of your core take shape as a flame,
flickering softly and brightly.
Feel this warm flame glowing within
as your awareness dwells only on this light.

Notice how your light streams in every direction,
desiring to grow, expand, and create more light.
Allow your light grow outward.
Feel it beaming wider,
spreading outward like a warm, white fire over your physical body.
Breathe it through you and over you
until you can feel yourself exist as a single white flame
flickering, weightless and warm.

Journey

Find yourself strolling along a path lit only by the light of the brilliant full moon. The evening air is pleasant, yet the silhouettes of the trees against the bright moon brings a sense of mystery to your journey along this path. Something exciting is about to happen. You can feel a texture of excitement in the air as you walk.

The evening path lit by the light of the moon is solid under your feet. The moonlight is your guide as you walk forward and you feel safe. The solitude and quiet is comforting and enjoyable.

On the ground in front of you, a tiny white pebble sparkles in the moonlight. You stop to reach down and pick it up. Examining it closer, you realize this pebble has absorbed the light of the moon and shines on its own. It is intriguing; smooth, round, and full in its appearance. It radiates an energy that is happy and makes you smile.

You decide to take the pebble along for your walk and give it meaning by making it a symbol of some part of you that already brings you joy. Something you are already experiencing now. Something that makes you feel full and joyful. You put it in your pocket for safe keeping.

Along the path, you begin to notice a few more pebbles glistening on the ground. These pebbles shine with many different colors. All very beautiful, but some more attractive to you than others. Each beautifully placed at your feet, you bend down to choose only the ones that bring you happiness. As you hold them in your hand, they are smooth, round, and full like the first. You reflect on how, in collecting them, you are gathering the pieces of your own joy.

Each pebble symbolizes something in your life that makes you feel whole. You give thanks and place them in your pocket.

You continue your travels and come to a part of the path where the ground is littered with dull gray pebbles. These pebbles do not shine with light. They have not adsorbed the moonlight like the others. Somehow you know they belong to you. You acknowledge which ones belong to you and gather them up.

Dark and gray in color, they are void of energy. They symbolize those things you have been searching for, things that will help you feel whole but have not yet come into fullness.

You assign each of them something that is missing from your life. Each to represent something that will bring you into wholeness and feel more complete. And when you are finished, you place them in your pocket.

Your walk soon takes you to a lake, where the full moon reflects brilliantly on the serene and still water. You stand on the shore of the lake with your pebbles in your pocket and take in the fullness of the moment.

Breathing in the full energy of the moon, you take the pebbles out of your pockets and lay them in a pile on the ground. You notice again that some pebbles are brightly shining, and others are dull and without luster.

You step up to the lake and look into the still water. The full moon is powerful yet soft, sitting like a gentle giant in the sky. You look into the lake, and your reflection reveals something unsettling. Your reflection is not complete. Only some parts of you are glowing and can be seen. Other parts of you cannot be seen as brightly or are missing altogether.

You reflect on why this is and turn to the pebbles in your wisdom. Each pebble is a part of you that contributes to your wholeness.

Each one represents something that brings you joy and closer to fullness. Some glowing, some dull. You gather up the ones that do not shine, the dull and lifeless ones, and you reflect on what joy are you keeping from yourself. What things, that qualities will bring you into fullness? And as you throw each one into the shimmering water, you declare they are now yours, and you deserve to feel whole, full, and complete!

Suddenly, three mysterious women rise up from the lake and shine brightly in the moonlight. Each woman a part of you … and your wholeness of being.
The first represents you healthy and physically whole.
The second represents you in mind, intellectual and creative.
The third is you spiritually and emotionally.
Three pieces of you coming together before you.

Here, they have come to collect your dull, lifeless pebbles and awaken the energy within them. They swim and gather all the pebbles that have sunk into the lake. They mesh them together to create one solid sphere and lift the sphere up to the moon. The moonbeams shine brightly down, illuminating the sphere as it absorbs the light, becoming brighter and brighter, bigger and bigger, energized and full and whole.

All the pieces that were missing and keeping you from feeling whole are now together in one sphere and shining brightly as the women hold it high above the water.

Together, the women walk out of the lake and hand you the complete and whole sphere of light. As you hold this sphere, you notice how easy it is to carry and how it resonates a vibration fulfillment. You give thanks to the women for their help and thanks to yourself for your courage in this endeavor.

Journey's End Reward

Looking into the lake once again, you can see your reflection in its entirety. Full, whole, and complete. Each part of you brilliantly reflected in the water.

You look to the moon and align yourself with its powerful energy as the moonbeams shower down. At the center of your being, you hold your sphere of light and are filled with the wholeness and abundance the moon reflects.

You thank the wise women who helped you gather your missing pieces and bring you wholeness as they disappear under the water of the lake.

You turn to walk back along the path, making your way back to this space and time, holding your sphere of joy and wholeness. Breathing deep and relaxed, you come back slowly, bringing all the energy of fulfillment and completeness with you. Let that feeling come into your lap as you energetically hold the sphere of light. Keeping your eyes closed, bring the energy of the sphere up to the top of your head. Let it melt into your head and soak into your mind. Let this energy and light release you from any doubt and any obstacles and affirm you in claiming your fullness!

Place your hands in prayer position over your heart and breathe. Feel your expansion.

Breathe in the fullness of your being
and give thanks.

Breathe yourself fully back and feel yourself where you sit.
Open your eyes, feeling good in every way.
Go in peace and dare to soar.

How did the dull rocks feel to hold in your hand? What specifically did they represent for you?

_____

_____

_____

_____

What would life be like if you were living in the fullness of your being? What does that mean to you?

_____

_____

_____

_____

What can you start doing right now that would help you feel more fulfilled, whole, and complete?

_____

_____

_____

_____

Autumn Grace

Letting Go, Courage

Autumn reminds us of how easy it is to let go. With a graceful acceptance, the trees willingly release their hold on what no longer serves them and transition forward. In this simple act of release, there is great wisdom and benefit. Too often and for much too long, we tend to hold on to the things that seize to provide any good for us and become heavy with their weight. In our release, we open the way and make room for the renewed sense of well-being.

Packing Your Spiritual Backpack

What are you clinging on to that no longer has a benefit? And for what reasons?

_____

_____

_____

_____

How would it feel to let it go?

_____

_____

_____

_____

Setting Out
Relaxation

Close your eyes and settle in.
Feel your body become soft.
Feel your breath lull you into stillness
and gently surrender your entire being into peace.

Breathe.
Let your breath roll over you like a quiet stream of calm and relaxation.
Breathe in a flow of warmth and love from your head to toes.
Breathe that calm into your mind, and release any thoughts and negativity.
Breathe into your body; let your breath soothe your every muscle into rest.
And now breathe outward, into your aura.
Feel yourself sit in stillness, peace, and calm …
mind, body, and spirit.

So comfortable, so relaxed.
Letting go … moving forward, moving inward …
Making room to welcome in more good.
Bring your awareness inward and
Just rest in a space of blissful peace.

Journey

The colorful and quiet autumn woods unfolds at your feet. Tall trees line the path you walk and spread out deep, creating a colorful forest wonderland. Their leaves glisten with vibrant shades of red, orange, and gold as the sun shines through their branches and brings down a sense of excitement. This transformation into fall is so breathtaking, it is as though you are walking through a painted masterpiece.

You feel supported by the ground beneath you, sturdy and firm. Dried leaves crunch under your feet as you walk and breathing in the fresh air brings on feelings of freedom and joy.

The squirrels scurry about the woods, gathering their nuts in preparation for winter. Long-necked geese fly overhead, squawking their goodbyes as they head south to warmer weather.

All around you, the trees show signs of their graceful release. The air is filled with brilliant colors as their leaves elegantly dance their way down to the ground. You are nourished by the bright colors of orange, grounded by the reds, and empowered by the hues of gold.

The trees accept and allow a part of themselves to let go. Holding on too tight to something that no longer serves them does no good. Willingly, they gracefully let go, giving themselves to freedom.

You walk slowly and take in the release, breathing in and out. There is something to admire in the trees' easy acceptance of what is happening and how it is making room for so much good to come.

In this woodland wonderland, the trees nudge you, inspire you with a gentle encouragement to the same.

As you stroll through the woods, all the thoughts, judgments, and opinions you hold on to that no longer serve you begin to surface. You think of situations, people, and behaviors that have no benefit coming along any further with you on your journey.

Up the path, you come to a tall oak tree still green and laden with leaves. Its branches are overcrowded and dense with leaves struggling to be freed. The oak stands hunched over, heavy and drooping from the weight. Amid all the autumn beauty and transition, this one tree stands alone in hesitation and resistance.

You can feel a sadness in the air and a yearning to be liberated from the heaviness. You approach this tree with love and compassion, sitting yourself up against its trunk, empathizing with its struggle and you begin to think.

Like the tree, you have leaves of your own. There are things you are clinging to that no longer will serve you on your path forward. All of these things that you may have been holding on to for too long come to mind. You can feel their weight on your shoulders and back.

You imagine how different life would be if you could just accept them and let go. How in the graceful act of release, you would be opened to a renewed sense of balance and peace. You think about the positive effects of letting these things go and the benefit of experiencing a renewed feeling of well-being.

Wrapping your arms around the tree, you decide to help alleviate each other from the heaviness. Taking a very deep breath in, you pull up any fear, any resistance, any hesitation, and with your out breath, you expel it all out into the cool, crisp air.

You breathe in courage, acceptance, and grace. And breathe out once again all that you wish to release. You surrender now to the grace to letting it all go. Immediately you can feel a change in yourself, mind, body, and spirit. A lightness comes over you, easing your being as you make a well-deserved sigh of relief.

You look up to witness the leaves of the oak suddenly turn color ... greens to red, orange, and gold. Slowly one by one, the tree relinquishes its control and allows its leaves to join in on the elegant dance of color through the air. Down they fall and reach the ground.

You sit under the tree as the leaves collect in a pile all around you. You notice an instant change taking place in the tree. There is a shift in the posture of the tree where now it stands taller and straighter. Having let go yourself, you can relate to how much lighter the tree must feel after this release.

In your joy, you roll in the leaves and play around with a childlike joy. You stand up and turn to thank the tree and the rest of the woodland for its wisdom. You thank yourself for the courage to accept this change and go forward.

After giving the tree one more hug, you turn to walk back along the same trail that led you here.

Journey's End Reward

Along with the leaves. The tree has also let go of something even more wonderful. Acorns fill the path in abundance at your feet. These acorns, also released from the oak, are the seeds of the new to come. With excitement, you envision all the possibilities you have now opened to yourself by setting yourself free and letting go. You gather the acorns as a symbol of each new good thing to come and carry them down the path in your pockets.

Feeling light and at ease, you stroll the woodland path back to this space and time. Free from the heaviness and feeling so renewed, you carry with you the energy of the acorns. Gently and with grace, you return to this space in time wiser, lighter, and grateful. When you are ready, open your eyes and breathe.

How did it feel to finally let it all go?

_____

_____

_____

_____

What good things have you made room for in releasing your "leaves"?

_____

_____

_____

_____

Winter's Growing Light

Year's End, Staying in the Growing Light

Winter comes to teach us to embrace the darkness, our challenges, our fears; to be still, to listen, and to learn. Dark and challenging times remind us to stay aware of the growing light outside that is also growing within. In our focus of this light, we are led to our own personal spring, our hope, our renewal, and our joy and wholeness.

Packing Your Spiritual Backpack

What darkness or challenges (spiritually, emotionally, or physically) are you currently experiencing?

_____

_____

_____

_____

What light (gift, skills, hope) within this darkness would you like to see growing in the light over the next few months?

_____

_____

_____

_____

Write your intention for this healing journey from your answers above.

_____

_____

_____

_____

Setting Out
Relaxation

Breathe deep, close your eyes.
Open your hands with your palms facing each other and hold them a few inches apart.
Take notice of the nothingness between your palms and notice energetically the empty space.
Slowly allow a tiny flicker of light to grow between your palms; feel the warm in your fingers and hands as the light grows.
Now place your intention for what you want to grow within the darkness, into this light.
As the light flickers, it grows larger and larger.
And as it grows, it nurtures and brings life to your intentions.
From seemingly nothing, let the light grow along with your intentions.

Let the small flicker of light travel up your arms,
into your shoulders, and soak into the base of your neck.
Feel it warm and illuminating you as it travels down every vertebrae,
down to the base of your spine.
In the core of your being, this light ignites a flame that grows from a tiny flicker to warmly radiate throughout your entire body and mind.
As it travels, it carries your intentions for healing and love to every cell.

Bring the light into your lungs.
Follow the natural rhythm of your breath

and feel it roll over your body
and into your mind.
Each part of you is loosening,
relaxing,
letting go.
Allowing the peaceful flow to lull yourself into rest.
Calm and still.
Relaxing deeper and deeper.
Go quietly and peacefully within …

Journey

Envision a cool winter's morning. You take in the crisp, still air and watch as the silvery gray sky hovers above. A light snow falls gently from the silvery sky. Gracefully the snow flurries fall to the ground. Each snow flake revealing a special and unique beauty, reminding you of the beauty you experienced this past year.

As the snowflakes gather on the ground, you recall your many blessings and gleefully watch as the snow piles up in abundance all around you.

Putting out your hands out, you invite the snow to land gently in your palms. As each snowflake lands and quickly melts away, you are reminded of the grace in letting things go.

Like the snow in your hand, this year is also melting away and coming to an end.

With each snowflake that melts away, you reflect on what in your life you wish to also melt away.

You easily let go of that which you wish to release and in turn make room for the next good to come.

Here in this special and quiet place, winter has arrived in all its beauty and mystery.

Behind the silvery clouds, the light of the sun is hidden. You can barely feel its warmth but know it is there all the same.

A light wind blows the snowy clouds, and the sun's light nudges its way out from behind them.

You watch and feel as the sun shines brighter and stronger with each passing second. You put your face to the sun and feel the warmth. The sun climbs higher in the sky, and on the snowy ground to your side, you watch as your shadow grows with the rising sun. Your shadow stretches out far on the ground, stretching out farther than any other time of the year.

The sun seems to stand still in the sky as morning turns into midday and shines very bright. You look to your shadow and notice the dark outline of yourself. At this time of year, your shadow has grown to its fullest, and in its fullness there lies all your experiences of the past year.

Images of the year emerge within your shadow. It was a full year with so much good as well as its share of challenges. Looking deep into your shadow, you simply witness all the good along with all the dark or challenging times … and you can take comfort that made it through and give thanks for it all.

This is a time for reflection …
In all the challenges, what has this past year taught you?

What gifts has each challenge given you?

You can let go of the disappointments and any sorrow and try to see what they were here to teach. You can reexperience all the good and happy times and feel the joy.

Once again, you look to the sun. It makes its way into a late afternoon position in the sky. Your shadow, like this year, grows shorter and shorter.

Soon the sun sets, disappears, and you stand under a very dark winter night sky.

This is a peaceful darkness that makes you feel safe and comforted. This is the dark of the longest time of the year, yet it is the dark of new life, the dark of the universe from where new birth of light and hope emerges.

You stand in this darkness protected, connected, and nurtured. In the quiet and stillness, you can feel peace. Looking up into the sky, there is complete stillness complete blackness. Here you stand, very still.

You breathe deeply, letting your breath become slow, easy, and soft. You feel yourself begin to lift up off the ground and into the dark, still night. You travel upward into the sky and enter deep into the loving arms of the universe. You travel into her calming stillness, where she wraps you in her love like a cozy blanket and cradles you.

Here, you rest rocking gently in her arms.

The universe, like a mother holding a baby, comforts you into stillness.

In this stillness, there is much to learn, much personal growth to occur, and many gifts to gather. You reflect on the winter that has now begun. Wrapped in this heavenly blanket of love, you feel the universe wants the very best for you. This, the longest night of the year, has given you the opportunity to grow the light within once again.

You reflect on any darkness you are currently experiencing and ask yourself, "What is the darkness, and what is it here to teach me?"

You listen in stillness, begin to gain new knowledge and understanding of the presence of the dark, and learn.

And you ask yourself, "What light is growing in this darkness?""

And you reflect, for even in the darkest nights, there is always a glimmer of some light, so what light is growing for you?

Out deep in the universe, you can see a glimmer of light from a single star. It shines brightly in the distance. The light is faint and far, far away, yet it is still there. In this light grows the answers, the gifts, the personal growth and wisdom.

Even on this, the darkest time of the year, the presence of light still shines, no matter how small, and holds for you hope and goodness. Wanting all that the light offers, you drift closer and feel a faint warmth radiating from the star's light.

It grows bigger and bigger as you approach, and its warmth is getting stronger. It shimmers and twinkles, and you stop in awe to take in its beauty.

Suddenly the star releases its light to you, showering a flow of millions little speckles of light forward. Shimmering and sparkling, the light streams to you, in you, and you become enveloped in its glimmer. Taking in all this light, you too begin to shimmer within the darkness just like a star.

Here, you recall again the darkness you are experiencing …

What is the light that is emerging within your current darkness?

What are the gifts growing in that light? What hope is coming?

With new answers and new hope, you soon begin to drift downward through the darkness, shimmering brightly. Yourself aglow, letting the wind bring you safely down to earth. Feel your feet touch the ground, returned to your special outdoor place.

Even though it is still dark, you feel a new sense of safety and security. Each tiny flicker of starlight within you remains and will grow brighter and stronger.

Journey's End Reward

Through this winter, you can make a promise to let your own light guide you through any darkness, watch it grow, and stay focused of the gifts to come.

Here on the ground, you look again to the sky and watch as the night fades and the sun begins to dawn. The light rises slowly. The sky is less cloudy than the day before the sun feels a tiny bit stronger this day. It seems a little bit brighter as it rises to warm you. Brighter and brighter it grows until it is directly overhead. You are filled with warmth, with rays of love and hope.

After the dark night, the dawn delivers its promise of hope and renewal.

Turning to face to the sun, you take in that promise of renewal and hope.

Looking now to ground, you notice your shadow is shorter than it was the day before. In the presence of more light, the shadow and darkness shrink.

So make a wish for the spring to come …
In the growing light that shines within and without,
you can deeply feel the endless possibilities of hope.

With new knowledge, trust and sit peacefully in the stillness of the winter while rejoicing in the light growing in each new day.

Come gently and slowly back into the room.
Breathe.
Begin to feel your body in this space and time,
and when you are ready, open your eyes and stretch.

What is the light growing for you within the darkness?

_____

_____

_____

_____

How can you stay present and focused on the growing light throughout this winter?

_____

_____

_____

_____

Draw a symbol of your growing hope, light, and reward. Keep it with you daily.

_____

_____

_____

_____

What will be your hope and promise for spring?

_____

_____

_____

_____

About the Author

Christine Chiechi has been empowering her audiences and clients through her unique guided imagery meditations for over 25 years. As a Reiki Master, Hypnotherapist and Meditation Specialist she has brought real hope and seeds of change to those seeking a renewed sense of self and purpose. Her background in Education and Psychology lends wisdom and compassion to her writing. Her work as an Ordained Minister shows up in her writing as love for healing and helping others.

Her clients have experienced her writing as life changing and empowering and providing them with the confidence to see themselves though any challenge or hardship. With everything she write, Christine, walks with the reader on their personal journey with encouragement and hope. She writes to elicit hope, self determination, a sense of self love and confidence as each reader journies down the promising path to renewal and self discovery.

Printed in the United States
By Bookmasters